Anthems for Choirs 2

Edited by
PHILIP LEDGER

Preface

The two volumes *Anthems for Choirs 2* and *3* form a comprehensive collection for soprano and alto voices ranging from the 13th century to the present day. They are suitable for cathedral, church, school, women's, girls', and boys' choirs. Volume 2 is devoted to unison and two-part anthems whilst volume 3 comprises anthems in three or more parts and a set of five introits. Four new anthems have been specially commissioned from David Lord, John Rutter, Robert Sherlaw Johnson, and Phyllis Tate. With the exception of Christmas (most choir libraries already contain music for this festival) all seasons of the Church's year are represented in the collection. There are 24 anthems in each book.

The keyboard realizations in volume 2 are editorial and may be played on the organ, harpsichord, or piano; some dynamics, tempo indications, introductions, and vocal ornamentation have been incorporated into the text. Further information about individual anthems is to be found in the Appendix to each volume. Unless otherwise stated, English translations are by the Rev. W. M. Atkins.

I am most grateful to David Chadd, Charles Cudworth, Julian Rushton, Allan Tonkin, and many other friends for their advice and assistance in the preparation of these books.

Philip Ledger

Anthems for Choirs 1 for mixed voices (edited by Francis Jackson) is on sale.

© Oxford University Press 1973

Printed in Great Britain

Oxford University Press

Music Department 37 Dover Street London W1X 4AH

Index of Titles and Opening Lines

Where opening lines differ from titles the former are shown in italics.

Anthems suitable for unaccompanied singing are marked thus *
Anthems are for two-part singing unless otherwise stated.

Index of Composers

For sources and further information see Appendix, page 108.

Seasonal Index

1. BEATUS VIR

ORLANDUS LASSUS
(1530—1594)

2. OCULUS NON VIDIT

ORLANDUS LASSUS
(1530–1594)

3. DUO SERAPHIM

RICHARD DERING
(c. 1580 – 1630)

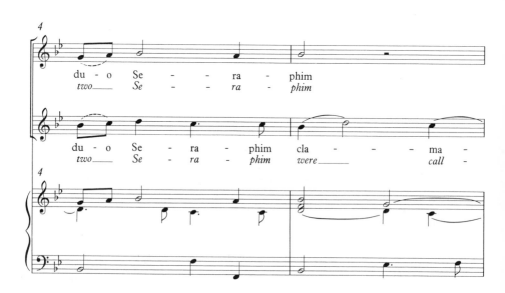

4. GAUDENT IN COELIS

RICHARD DERING
(c. 1580—1630)

5. EINS BITTE ICH VOM HERREN

HEINRICH SCHÜTZ
(1585 – 1672)

6. COME, YE CHILDREN

AGOSTINO STEFFANI
(1654—1728)

Come, ye chil - dren, and hear - ken to me,_____ I will

SOPRANO 1

SOPRANO 2

Come, ye chil-dren, and hear - ken to me,

7. CHRISTO RESURGENTI

FRANÇOIS COUPERIN
(1668—1733)

Note: the 'inequalities' or dotted rhythms should be 'lazy' in feeling (i.e. ♩♪ almost = ♩ ♪).

8. EVENING HYMN
(Unison)

WILLIAM FULLER

HENRY PURCELL
(1659—1695)

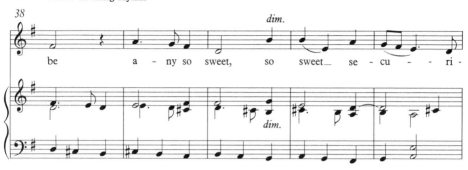

be   a – ny so   sweet,   so   sweet_   se – cu – – ri –

– ty!   Then   to thy   rest,_____   O ___ my

soul!   Then   to thy   rest,_____   O ___ my_

soul!   And sing – – – – – – – – ing praise   the mer - cy   that_

9. LORD, WHAT LOVE HAVE I

Psalm 119, v. 97

WILLIAM CROFT
(1678—1727)

10. WASH ME THROUGHLY

Psalm 51, v. 2

G. F. HANDEL
(1685—1759)

11. GIVE EAR UNTO ME

BENEDETTO MARCELLO
(1686 – 1739)

12. I WILL ALWAY GIVE THANKS

Psalm 34, v. 1

CHARLES KING
(1687 – 1748)

13. O COME HITHER

Psalm 66, vv. 14 & 17

MAURICE GREENE
(1695—1755)

14. THE LORD IS MY SHEPHERD

Psalm 23, vv. 1–3

MAURICE GREENE
(1695–1755)

15. O MY GOD, I CRY IN THE DAYTIME

Psalm 22, v. 2

JOHN REYNOLDS
(d. 1770)

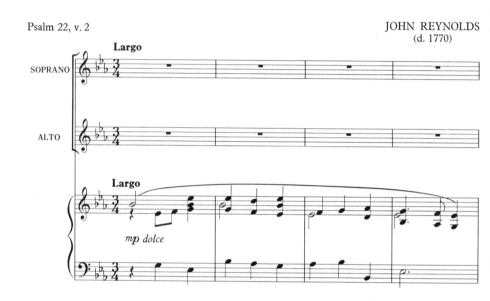

16. THE SORROWS OF MY HEART

Psalm 25, vv. 16 & 17

WILLIAM BOYCE
(c. 1710 – 1779)

17. STABAT MATER DOLOROSA

Tr. Beatrice E. Bulman

GIOVANNI BATTISTA PERGOLESI
(1710–1736)

18. THE SOULS OF THE RIGHTEOUS

Wisdom of Solomon III, v. 1

JAMES NARES
(1715–1783)

19. O SALUTARIS

English words by
Henry Coates

CÉSAR FRANCK
(1822 – 1890)
arranged by HENRY GEEHL

20. THE SONG OF THE TREE OF LIFE

(Unison or 2-Part)

Words adapted from
the Book of Revelation

R. VAUGHAN WILLIAMS
(1872–1958)

Note: This version differs slightly from the original stage version in the Morality *The Pilgrim's Progress.*
This anthem is published separately (T37).

© Oxford University Press 1952

21. LET SAINTS ON EARTH IN CONCERT SING

(Unison)

C. WESLEY
(1707—1788)

ALAN RIDOUT

1. Let saints on earth in con-cert sing___
2. One ar-my of the liv-ing God,___
3. Je-sus, be thou our con-stant guide;___

With those whose work is done;_____ For all the ser-vants
To his com-mand we bow;_____ Part of his host hath
Then, when the word is giv'n,_____ Bid Jor-dan's nar-row

of our King In earth_and heav'n are one._____
crossed the flood, And part_is cross-ing now._____
stream di-vide, And bring_us safe to heav'n.___

No. 4 of *Sacred Songs*

Reprinted by permission of Stainer and Bell Ltd.

22. LITANY TO THE HOLY SPIRIT

(Unison)

ROBERT HERRICK
(1591 – 1674)

PETER HURFORD

Andante e semplice

1. In ____ the hour of my dis - tress,
2. When ____ I lie with- in my bed,
3. When ____ the house doth sigh and weep,

23. SING WE MERRILY

Psalm 81, vv. 1—3

CHRISTOPHER SYMONS

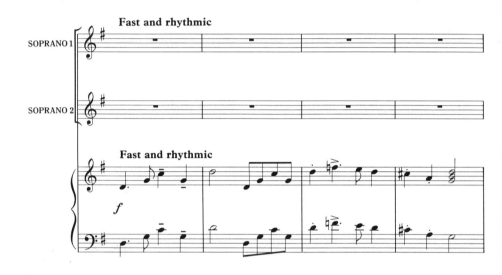

This anthem is published separately (E114).

© Oxford University Press 1968

24. CLOSE IN MY BREAST THY PERFECT LOVE

15th century anonymous words

DAVID LORD

This music is published by arrangement with Universal Edition (London) Ltd.

(Org. Man.)

Org. Ped. (Opt.)

(Org. Man.)

Processed and printed by
Halstan & Co. Ltd., Amersham, Bucks., England

Appendix

Sources and further information:

1. Beatus vir — Lassus
Novae aliquot et ante has non ita usitate ad duas voces cantiones suavissime ...
(London, Thomas Easte, 1598)
Note-values halved: transposed up a tone

2. Oculus non vidit — Lassus
Novae aliquot et ante has non ita usitate ad duas voces cantiones suavissime ...
(London, Thomas Easte, 1598)
Note-values halved

3. Duo seraphim — Dering
Cantica Sacra. Ad duas et tres voces composita
(London, Playford, 1662)
Note-values halved

4. Gaudent in coelis — Dering
Cantica Sacra. Ad duas et tres voces composita
(London, Playford, 1662)
Note-values halved

5. Eins bitte ich vom Herren — Schütz
Erster Theil Kleiner geistlichen Concerten ... In die Music versetzet Durch Heinrich Sagittarium (1636)
Note-values halved

6. Come, ye children — Steffani
Sacred Music for One, Two, Three and Four Voices ... arranged by R. J. S. Stevens
(London, for the Editor, 1803)

7. Christo resurgenti — Couperin
Versailles, Bibl. munic., Ms.59 ("Elevations de Couperin") freely arranged by the editor: second verse of the Latin text by Andrew Martindale, translated by the editor

8. Evening Hymn — Purcell
Harmonia Sacra: or Divine Hymns and dialogues ... composed by the best masters of the last and present age ...
(London, Playford, 1688)
Note-values halved

9. Lord, what love have I — Croft
Sacred Music for One, Two, Three and Four Voices ... arranged by R. J. S. Stevens
(London, for the Editor, 1803)
Note-values halved

10. Wash me throughly — Handel
Sacred Music for One, Two, Three and Four Voices ... arranged by R. J. S. Stevens
(London, British Museum, Ms. R.M. 20 d.7

11. Give ear unto me — Marcello
Sacred Music for One, Two, Three and Four Voices ... arranged by R. J. S. Stevens
(London, for the Editor, 1803)

12. I will alway give thanks — King
Sacred Music for One, Two, Three and Four Voices ... arranged by R. J. S. Stevens
(London, for the Editor, 1803)

13. O come hither — Greene
Sacred Music for One, Two, Three and Four Voices ... arranged by R. J. S. Stevens
(London, for the Editor, 1803)

14. The Lord is my shepherd — Greene
Sacred Music for One, Two, Three and Four Voices ... arranged by R. J. S. Stevens
(London, for the Editor, 1803)
Forty Select Anthems in Score ... Dr. Maurice Greene Volume 2
(London, Walsh, 1743)

15. O my God, I cry in the daytime — Reynolds
Sacred Music for One, Two, Three and Four Voices ... arranged by R. J. S. Stevens
(London, for the Editor, 1803)

16. The sorrows of my heart — Boyce
Fifteen anthems ... in score for 1, 2, 3, 4 and 5 voices
(London, 1780)

17. Stabat mater dolorosa — Pergolesi
Stabat Mater composed by Sigr. Pergolesi
(London, Walsh, 1740)

18. The souls of the righteous — Nares
London, British Museum, Add. Ms.19570

19. O salutaris hostia — Franck
O Salutaris (Messe Solemnelle)

20. The Song of the Tree of Life — Vaughan Williams
(London, E. Ashdown, 1959: two-part songs No. 246)
The Pilgrim's Progress: A Morality
(London, O.U.P., 1952)

21. Let saints on earth — Ridout
Sacred Songs (Set 1):
(Reigate, Stainer and Bell, 1965: Church Choir Library No. 639)

22. Litany to the Holy Spirit — Hurford
The Oxford Choral Songs U37
(London, O.U.P., 1958)

23. Sing we merrily — Symons
Oxford Easy Anthems E114
(London, O.U.P., 1968)

24. Close in my breast thy perfect love — David Lord
Commissioned for this volume